THE BOOK OF LASHONDA
SEAN::ADRIAN::BRIJBASI

Published simultaneously in the United
States and Great Britain in 2020
by Pretend Genius
Copyright © Sean::Adrian::Brijbasi

This book is copyright under the Berne
Convention
No reproduction without permission
All rights reserved

ISBN: 978-0-9995277-7-1

other books by Sean::Adrian::Brijbasi

One Note Symphonies
for Emma

Still Life in Motion
*for those who play
Marius and Andréus*

The Unknowed Things
for Julius

The Dictionary of Coincidences, Volume i
for Emma

S{E}AN?
for EM{M}A+

E{M}MA+ the ghost orchids
for Emma

darling two hearts
for E{M}MA+ the ghost orchids

Stories for Nadira
*for Adrian, Andréus, Elijah, Helena, Julius, Marius,
Nadira*

Play Championship World-Class
Tennis with Bjorn McEnroe
*for Adrian, Andréus, Elijah, Helena, Julius, Marius,
Nadira*

The World That Destroyed the World
*for Adrian, Andréus, Elijah, Helena, Julius, Marius,
Nadira*

Illustration

by

Helena Brijbasi

for
Adrian
Andreus
Elijah
Helena
Julius
Marius
Nadira

Chapter 1	1
Chapter 2	5
Chapter 3	9
Chapter 4	13
Chapter 5	19
Chapter 6	25
Chapter 7	31
Chapter 8	37
Chapter 9	41
Chapter 10	47
Chapter 11	53
Chapter 12	59
Chapter 13	63
Chapter 14	69
Chapter 15	75
Chapter 16	79
Chapter 17	85
Chapter 18	91
Chapter 19	95
Chapter 20	101
Chapter 21	107

"…if this was the year before

The year of disappearing, just until dusk

Just until the sidewalk ends

And love drifts to sleep…"

--Nadira Roberts

Chapter 1

1. Lashonda has no soul. She says it with the perspective of a detached observer.

2. She says it with a vaguely indelible context, the vagueness of which, over time, becomes more indelible than the context itself.

3. "I have no soul."

4. Perhaps she has the elements of (what seems universally imagined to be) a soul—

5. like a diabetic has the machinery of insulin-intake without the insulin required to fill human cells with the energy for life.

6. She's heard (or imagined she's heard) from people who might be described as ladies and gentlemen of ever-climbing aspirations

7. that the thus-far-unplumbed outskirts of some piece of music or poem or painting (quote-unquote) feeds their souls—

8. a note, a couplet, a concentration of colors, blurred to the vision (if it can be so called) of human beings by the daily-life-smudged spectacles of existence or muted

9. by the drumbeat of endless days of drab routine but nonetheless felt

10. like the intense blossoming of a flower, petals strained in all directions, to receive anything and everything

11. before the remaining light goeth-away and a barren darkness cometh-down.

12. Perhaps Lashonda has thought and even said much the same as she was being overcome

13. by some entity or feeling—an unutterable representation of a salubrious

excess that moved from somewhere inside her body

14. to outside (two or three inches) beyond her beautiful, pulsating skin, so that she felt as if she were, for a moment or even longer, unbounded

15. and for that very same moment or even longer as helpless as a baby bird but unafraid.

16. On the day she went to bury her book between the two birch trees in the woods behind her home

17. it rained, and she slipped down the slope of the hill and into the crevasse where she remained until she was found,

18. her white dress soaked through so that the children who found her saw her naked body as it might have been seen in a dream—

19. wrapped in a translucent cloud come down from the firmament—

20. softened, strangely alive, and unforgettable.

Chapter 2

1. Of the children who found Lashonda's body, a boy remembered her lying on a bed of flowers

2. and (from the moment he saw her) the words "queen of flowers" played in his head,

3. sometimes in his own voice and sometimes in the voice of his mother or father.

4. Sometimes in the voice of a stranger—an old element ("queen of flowers") and a new (the voice of a stranger)

5. merging across his synapses, expressing the combination of words and sounds in a way never expressed before.

6. As he grew older, he liked thinking of the words in a different voice

7. until the novelty wore off and he would use yet another voice with which to think of the words

8. or return to a voice he had not used in a long time (perhaps years), sometimes even his own.

9. He was easily distracted by the voices of people, having trained his ear over time to listen closely to the sounds,

10. if not the words, of those who conversed around him, so much so, that often

11. the words disappeared into the sounds that transported them and the entire structure

12. upon which was built his understanding of the language he spoke collapsed into a profound meaninglessness.

13. On occasion, and this was very rare, when he thought of the words "queen of flowers",

14. he also thought of the word "Lashonda" (almost in a whisper and in another voice,
15. as if it were in the background—a duet for violin and cello),
16. though it was difficult for him to get the harmony just right.
17. He had learned of her name from an article in the newspaper
18. about a previously unpublished book (*The World That Destroyed the World*) she had written
19. and for which she enjoyed (at the time of his reading) a small amount of posthumous ("some things are born posthumously")
20. fame.

Chapter 3

1. Of the children who found Lashonda's body, a girl remembered the white sheets of paper

2. strewn halfway down the slope of the hill, forming a path to Lashonda,

3. both physically as material substance like pavestones leading to her tangible existence (her legs, her face, her hands)

4. and metaphysically as immaterial substance, the story told on those sheets of paper, leading to her intangible existence (her mind, her being, her soul),

5. either incomplete without the other so that she was only ever known to one person,

6. who nevertheless mumbled (to the stranger sleeping next to him) as the bus passed the entrance of the Flower Viewing Garden,

7. "I knew her but I didn't understand her", though still better than others,

8. who considered her their closest friend and who would have felt shame in their hearts

9. had they read her story, that not only did they not understand her, but they never knew her at all.

10. The white sheets of paper held the girl's gaze in the opposite direction (away from Lashonda)

11. as if they were the arm and hand of her father pointing her away from a place

12. she shouldn't be (where other grown-ups she didn't know walked towards),

13. and in the direction of her mother, standing at the top of the hill,

14. who called her in a voice both commanding and reassuring ("come Lelolah"),

15. to guide her away from any danger without making her aware of the danger itself.

16. When she was older (at a precise age) she thought the face of all old mothers (unlike old fathers),

17. shared a resemblance, having been wrought by the combination of a genetically constructed

18. suffering—fear for those to whom they gave birth—and time.

19. And though she never saw Lashonda's face or knew whether Lashonda was the mother of any children,

20. she could look at her own mother and modulate the contours and lines of her face

21. to imagine what Lashonda would look like if she were still out there in the world somewhere.

Chapter 4

1. Of the women and men who danced at Lashonda's party,

2. a woman realized years later that she had become a part of Lashonda's history,

3. even more so than many others who would remind her, whenever the incident came up in casual conversation—

4. forgetting she was also there—that they saw her living body

5. the night before her other body was found and that it was (quote-unquote) senseless,

6. a tragedy, and though they didn't know Lashonda well she seemed like a decent person.

7. The woman couldn't have known that she might have become an even bigger part of Lashonda's history

8. as Lashonda had written in her book about an event, in which she was involved,

9. that occurred in the city only a few years before but decided after fretful deliberation

10. to remove the passage because as affecting as the event was to think about in the closeness of her mind or to tell in the open air,

11. the words that she used to write the story of the event (on those white sheets of paper found strewn around her body)

12. seemed unessential and she wanted to write only what was essential,

13. distilling her life into the strongest proof of what it meant (for her) to be human

14. in this strange world so that others might drink of it slowly and carefully (with care), if it were to their taste,

15. and perhaps extrapolate from her brief and apparently meaningless existence, the entire universe.

16. To do otherwise would have them in a drunken stupor unable to make sense

17. of what it was they were reading and dismiss everything

18. as a muddle of disconnected words stirring, in the vein of cut-rate sentiment, their most primal instincts.

19. Lashonda told the story at her party to a group of people in the kitchen and the woman was surprised to hear her name

20. enunciated (there was no mistake) as an historical figure of some significance as to the conflict, resolution, and denouement of the event.

21. She had heard stories before (little adventures Lashonda called them)

22. but they all seemed in Lashonda's distant past, a different life from a long time ago—

23. events, situations, and incidents that described a person of escapades,

24. both unfettering and precarious, the likes of which would never happen again.

25. But to hear that she played a part in one of Lashonda's little adventures

26. opened up the world to her in a way that made her feel a little braver.

27. Lashonda called them little adventures because to any observer it appeared as if nothing was happening—

28. perhaps someone reading alone on an otherwise empty bus,

29. or walking quietly beside another person,

30. or riding on the back of a motorcycle that disappeared beyond the curve of a darkening boulevard,

31. but reading, walking, and riding towards a beautiful unknown—the conversations, noises, and silence around her,

32. coalescing as a discordant symphony accompanying her tension-filled goings-on.

Chapter 5

1. Of the crowd that gathered to watch the paramedics take Lashonda's body away,

2. a girl among them saw a locket hanging down from Lashonda's neck as they lifted her up by her legs and shoulders

3. to place her onto the gurney and into the back of the ambulance,

4. the opening of which was, although similar as an entrance and exit in practice to other openings, ominously different.

5. The girl touched her own locket given to her as a gift by her parents for her thirteenth birthday

6. (something small and precious, like her, they said) that she wore on a short silver chain and that nested snugly

7. within the suprasternal notch at the base of her neck as if it had,

8. over just a few months since the "most fun birthday party I ever had", carved the little groove itself.

9. The girl wondered what Lashonda kept in her locket—no one knew.

10. Lashonda never opened it to show anyone and when someone asked

11. she would simply follow her strategy for questions she did not want to answer

12. and soliloquize on matters related to baking (bread or cookies for example) or a baking outlier (pudding),

13. which made it clear to anyone, even if the locket was empty, no answer was forthcoming,

14. so that the possible contents of the locket naturally (as all things hidden) became a topic of conversation amongst her friends.

15. Could it be the photograph of a lover they didn't know? Her parents? Perhaps a drop of her own blood?

16. Some days she was ready to tell them but, on those days, they didn't ask or weren't around to ask

17. and she would unclasp the locket, remove it from her neck, hold it in the palm of her hand to feel its weight,

18. then think to herself that it was no heavier than the tiny, unhatched egg of a hummingbird,

19. a thought she kept on a short list of thoughts to think on her deathbed that she practiced

20. a few times a week (one, unclasp locket, two, remove from neck, three, hold in palm of hand, four, think thought—

21. "no heavier than the tiny, unhatched egg of a hummingbird")

22. so that it might instinctively come to her when the occasion arose.

23. The girl kept her sister's photograph in her own locket, who was not only her sister but her best friend,

24. as is the case with most siblings whose love was not built on the language of love (that she would come to crave,

25. for a few years in the future, from both men and women) but on love itself;

26. the love we feel for beings whose mechanisms for language are undeveloped (children) or non-existent (animals)

27. and who we continue to love as if it were always so.

28. Lashonda also had a sister, the person for whom her book *The World That Destroyed the World* was written,

29. though some passages were left out because several pages of the manuscript were made illegible by the rain.

30. A secret world existed behind the world Lashonda described in her book

31. and the missing pages imparted the location of several consequential landmarks—

32. the dress shop, for example, where she bought all her dresses,

33. including the one she wore (her favorite white chiffon) on the day her body was found.

Chapter 6

1. On the afternoon before the night of her party Lashonda took a shower

2. and instead of using her hands to wash her hair let the water commit itself fully—

3. without human intervention and (further removing, from its customary interaction,

4. any sub-atomic chemical liaison with her luxury shampoo and conditioner molecules)—

5. to the act of bonding alone (at last) with her hair follicles and the scalp from which they grew

6. in such a way that heightened, perhaps even maximized, the sensation of wetness

7. around her head and face, a landscape which remained as unmoved

8. by the torrent as a wall of rock beneath cascading falls,

9. so that the water surged untamed, attaching itself to loose smidgens

10. trapped in the approximately two-hundred-thousand hair shafts on her head,

11. transporting the smidgens downward, beginning from a great height as seen from below,

12. at her forehead, over her face, her nose, her neck (from which she had removed her locket

13. to hang on the little doorknob of the medicine cabinet door),

14. the space between her breasts, through the intermammary cleft,

15. her stomach, turning at the naval, along the crest of her hip,

16. the side of her thigh, behind her knee, to her calf, her Achilles, the base of her heel,

17. and finally onto the shower floor, into the small black hole of the drain, and from there to an unseen world.

18. She thought that perhaps one day the water would return to her (smidgen-less) and she would know

19. (in her being) that it was the same water from the shower on the afternoon of day/month/year,

20. filtered and cleaned, but at its core and in its essence the very same—

21. in the neighborhood swimming pool, at a drinking fountain in a school or park,

22. from the faucet at a friend's house, maybe even from the sky itself, drawn up from the earth and returned as rain.

23. Lashonda, the identifier of same water—any water that had ever touched her body.

24. Even the single drop that hit her eyelash as she waited out the downpour

25. beneath the striped awning of her favorite brasserie just yesterday eve,

26. she would identify some-number-of years later in the tea she shared with a companion,

27. or from the puddle she stepped into after saying good-bye to someone she loved

28. but would never see again, and which soaked through her shoe and sock (all the way) to her foot,

29. so that the beauty and sadness of their goodbye would forever be linked to the distress of her wet toes.

30. On the morning she was found, the water that adhered to her cheek,

31. as the rest of the water flowed off her body to be replaced by other water,

32. had travelled "far and wide" over "time and space" to reunite with her (it would not let her go),

33. starting its journey on the day she was born when the delivery nurse wet the sponge

34. laid out by the delivery nurse's assistant to clean off the residue of a difficult birth (beginning with her forehead)

35. before her first sleep in the alien world into which she had been so suddenly and violently pushed.

Chapter 7

1. Of the people Lashonda invited to her party she told a few of them they could sleep at her house

2. which for her was extraordinary and perceived by the invitees as more of a request than a courtesy.

3. She had a spare bedroom that two or more of them could share, a sofa,

4. and floor space behind the sofa on which she could lay out a soft blanket.

5. And (even more extraordinary) she wrote—word for word to each of them—

6. "I will provide an extra pillow as a buffer against the wall if you sleep in the space behind the sofa".

7. The last person Lashonda saw sleeping was her sister, many years ago before her sister disappeared.

8. Perhaps she saw a friend sleeping when she was a teenager though the memory was vague,

9. so that she was only certain of ever seeing her sister sleeping, whose breathing

10. she checked in the darkness of their room, made even darker by the black curtains

11. put up by their mother so that the girls might sleep through the night undisturbed

12. by light from the moon or the flickering from passing cars.

13. Lashonda would lean in closely (but not too closely so as not to wake her sister)

14. until she heard the exhalations of air from her sister's lungs,

15. which were always more perceptible than the inhalations (inferred)

16. until she was satisfied (minutes later) that her sister was alive and well

17. before taking the two or three steps backwards to her own bed
18. to lie down and wonder if, after she fell asleep, her sister woke up to watch her and check her breathing also.
19. She surmised that her sister did because on some mornings
20. when she woke up, she saw that the curtains had been parted,
21. not all the way, but enough to see the top of the tree outside their window and the sky above it
22. so that it was a simple exercise for anyone to imagine from the vertical breach
23. created by the curtain-parting, the horizontal expanse that stretched on either side of the thick, black fabric.
24. Lashonda only thought years later that her sister lay awake at night or at dawn

25. looking over her sleeping body and out through the window—to imagine what, she didn't know.

26. She had a strange feeling (sadness?) when she thought about the parted curtains of their room

27. but couldn't be certain if the feeling was rooted in what she was remembering,

28. blended and inseparable from the successive acts of opening her eyes, seeing her sister sleeping,

29. turning her head towards the window to see if the curtains had been parted (or not), and seeing them parted,

30. or a new feeling, with its own roots, in search of a memory in which to plant itself, and strengthened each time

31. by the briefest reminiscence, the merest glimpse by her mind at the memory of the parted curtains.

32. She told a friend that the feeling, which began as a mild complaint, had grown into a full-blown malady,

33. feeding on her memory, and sometimes subduing her in her own living room so that although

34. she went through the trouble of taking a shower, dressing herself in clothes she laid out the night before,

35. and putting on her shoes to go out into the world somewhere, she (instead) sat on her sofa and ended up going nowhere.

36. The friend she spoke to about her malady was one of the people she invited to sleep at her house

37. but who went home (like all the others) when the party finally ended.

38. Lashonda thought afterwards that if she had known they weren't going to stay she would have made an announcement

39. during the party that anyone who wanted to stay, even those she had not invited to stay,

40. were welcome to find a cozy spot around her house somewhere (anywhere) and fall asleep.

Chapter 8

1. It can be said that Lashonda wrote her book *The World That Destroyed the World* with a propulsion unfamiliar to her

2. regarding any other goings-on she had ever been involved with.

3. Every morning she woke up early not knowing what would come next

4. but knowing (if it can be called knowing) that if she sat at her desk

5. and thought of nothing and did nothing that she would think of something

6. and that something would happen so that whatever came next,

7. came as naturally as her perception of the flow of time represented

8. by the wall clock's second hand which moved without being interrupted

9. by the mechanical pause between the seconds seen in those fancy clocks
10. sold at the local clock store (where on many rainy days she devoted too much time
11. perusing the different clock styles and their interior apparatus),
12. so that she could see time elapsing at its most infinitesimal units.
13. She thought of the clock as her body, the seconds eaten up by the second hand as the cells in her body
14. and the infinitesimal units eaten up within the seconds as the molecules and atoms in her cells.
15. If there were units more infinitesimal to be eaten up then she saw those eaten up too.
16. On the morning after her party she woke up and sat down at her desk

17. as she always did and continued writing—she was near the end of her book—

18. describing, in the final paragraph of the final chapter (there was only one),

19. how the main character floated on his back on a slow-moving river and looked up to the trees above him.

20. She had been writing since university and there was always a voice inside her head

21. when she reread what she wrote until recently when she would reread what she had written

22. and realize there was no discernible voice that accompanied the words

23. as if water had learned how to speak and spoken the words she had written

24. as ebb and flow on a riverbank, a current over small rocks and broken twigs,

25. or a surge against a sea wall upon which people sat together to look out

26. to the sea and the horizon, sometimes as the sun rose, sometimes as it set.

27. She wondered that if she were not writing a book whether she would have thought of the clock as her body

28. or if she would have just stared at the second hand go round and round.

29. She conjectured that she might as well have thought of a stapler as her body

30. or, less unseemly, a fridge, with the food inside the fridge

31. (for example, the cheese, the eggs, and, in particular, the olives)

32. as the cells of her body, cooked first if they were raw, seasoned to taste, and eaten up by her.

Chapter 9

1. In her book *The World That Destroyed the World*,

2. Lashonda wrote about the disappearance of her sister

3. who she described as male instead of female to give readers (though at the time she had none)

4. the impression that the book was about someone else and not her,

5. but the book was about her and how she felt about her sister's disappearance,

6. who was younger and who she cared for as a mother might care for a child.

7. A child she worried "sick" about, a child she protected from danger (real and perceived),

8. and, like any mother, a child for whom she wanted a long life but from whom she felt

9. she would have to ask forgiveness (forty or fifty years later)

10. as she watched her walk unsteadily into the kitchen for a cup of tea,

11. stopping every few seconds to brace herself against the counter and find her breath;

12. the same kitchen she ran into as a little girl for candy on Saturday afternoons,

13. because while she had done everything to care for her sister and protect her from danger (real and perceived)

14. so that she did live a long life, she couldn't protect her from growing old

15. and from the physical pain of the different parts of her body,

16. or the mental pain of the different parts of her brain—

17. the pain of forgetting and remembering, good memories and bad,

18. memories which Lashonda herself dove into but couldn't swim in,

19. couldn't splash around in, and which forced her body

20. to drift along the surface, beyond her control, on its back

21. so that she could only look up to the trees and the sky to try and catch

22. a reflection of what it was she felt all around her skin but couldn't see.

23. She thought rainy days were best because she might glimpse

24. something about her sister reflected in a falling rain drop

25. or on the underside of a wet leaf on a low hanging branch or

26. if the raindrops were close enough together—a dense drizzle—

27. then she might be able to see a memory of her sister whole,

28. even if it was only the reflection of a memory misshapen by waves,

29. obscured by leaves, or deformed by the rain itself.

30. On the morning that she went to bury her book between the two birch trees behind her house

31. she still had hope that her sister would return and that she wouldn't have to imagine

32. what she would look like forty or fifty years from now

33. or, in forty or fifty years, try to remember her forty or fifty years ago, although her friends

34. who jokingly called her hopeless because she was always late or because she spent hours

35. at the grocery store without buying a single grocery stopped using the word around her.

36. She might say that she still had hope but unknown to them or to anyone else

37. she had started a mental list of shiny objects that might reflect what was around her just in case:

38. a low flying airplane, a balloon caught in the branches of a tree,

39. a piece of glass carried by a crow as it flew across the river.

Chapter 10

1. Before the sun rose on the morning that Lashonda's body was found

2. her neighbor saw a light on in Lashonda's house that, if he had been awake at the same time

3. every morning, he would have seen, so that on the morning he saw the light on in Lashonda's house

4. for the first time he would not have thought it strange for someone

5. to be awake so early simply because it was strange for him.

6. But he had been awakened by a dream that morning.

7. In the dream he walked around his house which transformed as he walked

8. into an open space to the ocean, or the onset of the ocean,

9. not the ocean fully realized—something ocean-like

10. with remnants of objects that were furniture-like—adjacent to his living room,

11. a part of the house that led to the house itself that should have been external

12. to the setting in any other setting but in his dream situated perfectly where it (sometimes) was.

13. And yet somewhere in the barely conscious part of his brain he felt unnerved,

14. as if he had spilled a blob of red hot sauce on his favorite red shirt (his only one)

15. so that he could feel the blob of red hot sauce moistness on his chest

16. even though no one else could see it unless he had explicitly told them

17. and pointed to it ("right here") without touching it.

18. And not just feel it on his chest but taste the hotness of it in his mouth

19. even though on the landscape of his body, one could say—

20. if the body is, as it is so often described, a planet of an eastern galaxy—

21. that his chest and his mouth were thousands (and on some planets, millions) of miles apart.

22. It was this dream that woke him and moved him from his bed to his bedroom window

23. through which he saw the shadow of what could only be Lashonda cast on her curtains

24. (though it provided only a vague translation of her movements behind it)

25. bending down perhaps, walking back and forth across the room,

26. lifting her arm or both arms up (he couldn't be sure),

27. then disappearing, only to return and walk back and forth across the room again.

28. And then as it began to rain, he saw a part of her face

29. between the curtains like the one word a traveler might recognize

30. in the sentence of a foreign language (*toujours* or *sensucht*)

31. on the cover of a magazine in a hotel in Marseille or Berlin,

32. but only for a moment as if she heard tapping against the window glass

33. and peeked out to confirm what she thought she had heard—rain;

34. rain that invited her (as an identifier of same water) to leave her house just fifteen or twenty minutes later

35. to go bury her book between the two birch trees in the woods.

36. He might have followed her if he had seen her (in her white chiffon dress)

37. but he had gone back to bed and gotten up later that morning

38. unable to remember the dream that woke him up in the first place.

Chapter 11

1. As the bus passed the gates of the Flower Viewing Garden, Lashonda's friend spoke out loud,

2. though still a mumble, words that the man sleeping next to him wouldn't hear and the people

3. awake around him couldn't put into (the) context of someone whose name they didn't know—

4. Lashonda: *I knew her but I didn't understand her.*

5. They might understand the sentence he mumbled and the idea

6. being (or trying to be) communicated by the sentence because everyone knows

7. or knew someone they don't or didn't understand, although it's possible that those rarest of human beings

8. understood or understand everyone they've ever known, know now, and will ever know.

9. Nevertheless, it was his way of trying to make sense of what happened to (or with?) Lashonda

10. (though he might not have known it) through the use of words that released the memories

11. in his brain so that perhaps he would gain an understanding (though not in the nimblest of ways)

12. of the peculiar circumstances of that morning: *I knew her but I didn't understand her.*

13. The involuntary repetition of the words in his brain after their unexpected vocalization,

14. impelled by the truest feeling he'd ever had—helplessness,

15. might (he surmised) knock a full memory box—or at least a trinket backpack—

16. off the "shelf of his hippocampus" (as the doctors say) and spill its contents bare

17. onto the floor so that during the act of returning everything to the box (or backpack)

18. he would see something—a hair clip, a sentence from a letter, a gesture—that would give him pause

19. and lead to something else in another box (or backpack) so that box by box (or backpack by backpack)

20. a narrative would form from the bits and pieces that fell from *theres-in*

21. so that he would be able to make sense of at least one thing—*a* one thing or even *the* one thing—

22. and be reconciled in his mind about the beautiful and enigmatic being who was Lashonda.

23. I knew her but I didn't understand her: nothing.

24. The words tumbled around in his brain (tin on tin inside of tin) as the bus rumbled on

25. and when it stopped again in front of his favorite grocery store

26. it seemed to him that he was no longer thinking about Lashonda (for the time being)

27. but he could only observe what was going on outside of his brain and not inside

28. because the beauty and enigma of Lashonda became something like an iridescent dust

29. that sparkled in and around his thoughts and, in those moments when he had no thought or was thinking very little,

30. descended slowly into the different regions of his brain and settled there,

31. until stirred up again by other thoughts so that even his dumbest thoughts

32. from that bus-ride on (both of which there were many) had something of a shine to them.

Chapter 12

1. Lashonda had tried everything to protect her grief, while also trying to protect herself
2. from her grief, distracting herself with hobbies (gardening, baking, bicycling)
3. so that one, a few, or all of them might become absorbed by her being and dilute her grief
4. as a way of protecting it and protecting herself from it but people still asked her
5. how she was doing, still observed and told others how to observe evidence of her grief
6. in the way that she half-smiled or looked indifferently when they spoke to her—
7. "you can tell from her eyes that she's not happy" someone might say
8. or "she looks away when you're talking to her" another might say

9. as if they were great detectives of the human condition.

10. It seemed there was nothing she could do to protect her grief, which had become her base feeling,

11. and like some people whose feelings showed through in their every action or conversation

12. (even now one hears the words "she exudes nobility"),

13. she felt that her grief showed through in her every action or conversation

14. so that it was no longer her own as she was (violently—in her mind) disinclined to share it with anyone;

15. but her grief was like a sword that had been driven through the top of her skull,

16. straight down into her body, stuck there with edges that never dulled, piercing her flesh, organs, and bone,

17. transmitting fresh throbbing pain in all directions so that no amount of strawberries picked,

18. no amount of cakes or cookies baked, no amount of bicycling past the clock shop,

19. through the alley between her favorite brasserie and the fan shop (owned by the old lady from Ishikawa prefecture),

20. to the path beneath the arching laburnum along the river,

21. where the man who fished from the bridge every morning mistook Lashonda's gesture

22. of reaching up to touch the yellow flowers hanging from the branches above her

23. as a wave and waved back to her (though she never saw him),

24. could contain or mask her grief, making it seen and sometimes felt by all the people around her who cared.

25. At home where she didn't have to mask her grief she would lie down anywhere—

26. on the bed, in the bathtub, on the kitchen floor, on the grass in her backyard—

27. and repeat her sister's name over and over again in her head so that she felt her sister's name

28. flow into the skin of her face (like a ghost), changing the shape of her eyes,

29. the slope of her cheeks, the form of her chin and lips, until little by little—

30. if she repeated her sister's name often enough and without interruption—

31. she felt that her sister's face—as she would always remember it—had become her own.

Chapter 13

1. On the morning Lashonda's body was found, the man who fished

2. from the bridge above the river running through the 6 Cities

3. moved his eyes from the water to the bicycle path to see if the woman (Lashonda—unknown to him) he had seen almost every morning

4. on those almost-too-perfect spring days, rode by so that he would wave to her as she waved to him.

5. He had timed how long it took for her to ride from one end of the bicycle path

6. (from the moment she rode into his view) to the other (the moment she rode out of his view)

7. so that he knew how often he had to look up from the river to the path

8. to make sure that when the woman rode by and waved to him, she would not ride by without seeing him wave back to her,

9. which, in his mind—the absence of the return wave (a non-gesture)—would have left her

10. with the disorienting feeling of not being waved to by someone you have waved to first.

11. Her morning bicycle ride—or, magnified further: the anticipation of seeing her—

12. had caused some tension on his otherwise placid fishing mornings

13. as he was always anxious that she would ride by at the precise moment a fish nibbled on his hook

14. so that both of his arms would be occupied, leaving him unable to return her wave before she rode out of his view.

15. He thought that if, by bad luck, he did get a nibble as she rode by

16. he would exaggerate the movements of pulling on his fishing line

17. so it was obvious to the woman that he could not wave to her

18. as he was in the throes of reeling in the "big one" and she would therefore understand

19. that she should not wave to him in the first place.

20. The tension was always relieved, however, as soon as he saw her—her arm lifted toward the hanging yellow flowers of the laburnum—

21. and since he had started fishing from the bridge, the presence of the woman in his morning routine,

22. for reason or reasons unknown to him, filled him with a sense of calm and well-being,

23. which made him feel for those twenty or thirty seconds she rode by that all-in-all he had a happy life

24. or as happy a life as he could have under the conditions in which he (or anyone for that matter) was forced by life to live

25. and that the world itself which he (or anyone for that matter) was forced by life to live in,

26. whether it be the cause or effect (or both) of that life, was beautiful—after all—and should be blessed and not cursed.

27. He would catch himself at the end of those moments, however, after she rode out of his view

28. and wonder if he should allow himself to live too long in that maelstrom of bliss

29. which opened (unexpectedly) to him like a vast ocean behind a secret door,

30. and like a vast ocean, when seen from the shore, seemed endless, more ominous, and bigger than the world itself.

31. But Lashonda did not ride by that morning—perhaps it was the rain,

32. though she had ridden by on other rainy mornings—or the morning after that

33. or for the rest of the spring and into summer during which time he had gotten many nibbles and caught many fish.

34. He thought he would wave to her first the next morning she rode by—

35. maybe she had stopped riding by because he had never done so—

36. but thought again she might think him too presumptuous.

37. And though he would never see her again, and though those mornings occupied

only the thinnest sliver of his time in the world,

38. he would never forget the gesture of the woman waving to him as she rode by on her bicycle—

39. a strange thing to remember, a wave from a stranger—for the rest of his life and think about it often.

Chapter 14

1. It was a warm enough day in early spring for Lashonda to sit at one of the outside tables of her favorite brasserie,

2. beneath the striped awning and across from the fan shop owned by the old lady from Ishikawa prefecture,

3. where, unknown to the man and woman sitting at a nearby table,

3. she borrowed a phrase that was a creation of the conversation they (the man and woman) were having—

4. a phrase not said by one or by the other, a phrase which perhaps they (the man and woman) were not aware of

5. but which drifted on the gentle breeze of a Saturday afternoon-eve,

6. and offered itself up as a gift to anyone nearby who was listening.

7. The words from the end of one sentence (spoken by the woman)
8. and the beginning of another sentence (spoken by the man),
9. when compounded—though compounded or merged or any other word
10. for the unbothered bringing together of two airy things all seemed too harsh for the encounter—
11. affected Lashonda in a way she could not understand or explain.
12. She wrote the words down on a piece of paper (already on the table)
13. so she would not forget them and added the phrase created by them
14. to her shortlist of thoughts to think on her deathbed which she practiced
15. a few times a week with the other thoughts on her list—

16. for example, "no heavier than the tiny, unhatched egg of a hummingbird".

17. She had gone to the brasserie to write a letter to her sister (in the open air)—a letter for which she had no address—

18. that she would put in her desk drawer where she kept other letters she had written to her sister,

19. in which she would write only what she could say and not what she wanted to say,

20. because there was still a chance her sister would return after all these years

21. and to write what she wanted to say might in some way jeopardize her return.

22. She thought of the desk drawer she kept the letters in as the darkest circle within her dark circle,

23. a place where no one could reach her but still a place where, although she could be by herself,

24. she could not be herself because her self was not whole.

25. The man and the woman lowered their voices after Lashonda wrote on the paper

26. but she had already scribbled the words she heard them say (diagonally) above the letter's salutation

27. "my most deeply loved" that started the transmission (she liked to think of them as) to her sister

28. and in which followed words, sentences, and paragraphs that preserved the sense

29. that she was speaking to her sister, that her sister would return,

30. and that together they would go to the dress shop where she had just, over the past weekend,

31. bought the white chiffon dress that quickly became her favorite.

32. A heavier breeze blew in as she put her pencil in her backpack,

33. carrying the letter away and onto the ground by the foot of the woman sitting at the nearby table

34. who picked it up and turned to hand it to Lashonda and as she did

35. saw and read the words that Lashonda had scribbled at the top:

36. to tell you just tell me.

Chapter 15

1. Early in the morning on the day of the week before Lashonda's body was found

2. the man responsible for maintaining the good working order

3. of the bell in the town's bell tower—the clapper and clapper springs;

4. the bell yoke and shaft; the strike path to make sure the bell's ringing was "crystal clear"

5. as it reached the ears of all the people and animals who lived in the 6 Cities

6. and possibly those of the people and animals who lived on the hem of its outskirts—

7. saw Lashonda walking her bicycle in the middle of the road,

8. on which there were no cars or buses because (he could only surmise) it was too early.

9. From up there he could see the town in all directions and the only person

10. or animal or machine he saw between the maze of streets and buildings and trees

11. was Lashonda (person and animal) and her bicycle (machine).

12. He thought that if he rang the bell then the person walking the bicycle

13. would pause (he imagined the front bicycle tire turning to a stop on the asphalt) to look up to the bell tower,

14. which was in the distance (for her), while the bell rang—at such a strange hour?—

15. and maybe even ring the little bell on her bicycle (if it had one) in reply

16. before re-mounting and going on her way when the ringing stopped

17. to ride through the empty roads of the 6 Cities as the sun separated from the horizon

18. and the bell's aftersound lingered in the (French pronunciation) foyer of silence around her.

19. The previous year he had brought a friend with him to the 6 Cities

20. as a sort of field trip in which they would make a day of it

21. after he checked the bell (clapper, clapper springs, bell yoke, and strike path, etc.),

22. and who also had a bicycle (and long hair—it appeared) but with whom he was no longer friends

23. because she told him that, while she acted in a way to never inconvenience him,

24. he acted in a way to always give her the chance to show him that she liked him

25. and, although he was liked (for a little while) and generally likable,

26. she could not go on always showing him that she liked him and like him at the same time.

27. Still, when he thought back to the day they were together the previous year

28. he had a good feeling and searched in all directions for the café where they had lunch

29. when, at noon, they heard the bell ring and looked at each other and smiled.

Chapter 16

1. On the afternoon of the day that Lashonda's body was found
2. the Ghost Orchids played a concert in the Flower Viewing Garden,
3. that Lashonda did and did not want to go to because it was at a Ghost Orchids concert
4. she last saw her sister when they stood shoulder to shoulder
5. in the crowd and moved to the music until the penultimate song,
6. the very first note of which her sister told her (as if on cue) that she was going to talk to a friend
7. at the entrance of the Flower Viewing Garden and, whether she did or did not, never returned.
8. Lashonda looked for her everywhere, called her many times, went to her home

(and other searchable places) but her sister had vanished.

9. She couldn't figure out what happened to her sister and, after a few days,

10. called the police who also couldn't figure out what happened to her sister.

11. Weeks went by, then months, then years, during which time Lashonda

12. didn't listen to one piece of music and had become so wary of music

13. and its true intentions that if she happened to hear music, by chance,

14. coming from somewhere, she did whatever she could to block it out.

15. If it was nearby, she walked away; if it came from another room (and she had the power within her) she closed the door;

16. if it came on the radio, she turned the radio off;

17. and if she could not walk away or close the door or turn the radio off, she hummed to herself,

18. a single internal note, like a drone in her ears—deeper than her ears—that blocked out all other sound

19. until she was free from the music around her to continue doing

20. whatever it was she was doing if the will to do it had not quietly snuck off

21. while she was deaf to the world (at-large) around her and herself (at-small) inside her.

22. She thought that having a party the night before (with "sweet delicious music") would prepare her

23. to go to the concert and stand in the crowd (with maximum awareness of her surroundings),

24. where she and her sister stood, and wait—like she waited before—

25. for her sister to return from wherever it was she had gone off to.

26. Maybe something went wrong in the previous circumstance that when righted

27. would immediately (or more quickly) make her sister return and all could go on as before

28. so that all the memories of her sister would give her a good feeling again instead of a bad feeling

29. because it was only torment to remember her sister

30. and think that her life and the world she lived in was still meaningful,

31. and if it was still meaningful, feel good about the time she spent

32. with the person she loved most in this (meaningful) world.

33. Only meaningless memories kept her going (meaningful memories were no longer made)—

34. daffodils in early spring, the crescent sun on the back of a pinhole camera, the day she learned to ride a bicycle.

35. In the beginning, a second at a time, then a minute at time, then an hour

36. at a time, then a day at a time, until she could go no further.

Chapter 17

1. He didn't always follow directions—unusual behavior for his school—

2. which his teachers sometimes let him get away with (and when he did, get away scot-free),

3. so that when he left the esteemed halls of academia for good, the tendency to wander off had fully set in,

4. and if he had neglected to grease a pan so the muffins stuck

5. or meandered off the edge of a cliff and fallen hundreds of feet to his probable death,

6. no one, but the most perceptive sleuth, searching back years, would have found any clues as to the cause.

7. The message to all passengers was clear: the bus will leave without you,

8. but he had wandered off and gotten lost near Hanami Park and when he returned the bus was long gone.

9. He sat down on the steps outside of town hall to think about what he would do next

10. when he saw a girl taking photographs of the Cheval Gauvin fountain near the road.

11. He watched her and how she seemed unconcerned with her surroundings

12. and decided, without knowing what to say, that he would speak to her.

13. On his way he thought he would ask her about the fountain (a passable line of inquiry)

14. and what the sculpture of the horse rising from the water represented

15. but when he stood in front of her he could only manage to say "hi",

16. which was as pleasant (if not more than) anything anyone had said to her that day.

17. She asked him if she could take his photograph near the fountain (she took two)

18. and then they walked without knowing where they were walking,

19. deciding as they walked until they reached a park and sat down on a bench

20. to continue their conversation (a mental walk) about the characteristics

21. they each found interesting about themselves,

22. that others might also find interesting as their shoulders and arms touched,

23. all the way down to their elbows—an intimacy they both acknowledged and allowed

24. by looking away from each other and (for a few moments) remaining silent, he to catch his breath, she to think.

25. When they finally spoke again, she said she had to get back to her hotel—

26. it was getting dark and it was a long walk, if they could even find their way.

27. As they walked, he saw a row of motorcycles parked in front of a crowded restaurant.

28. He checked each one to see if someone had left a key in

29. and when he found one, turned it, and called the girl over

30. with a bend of his head as he twisted the throttle (just to hear the sound).

31. She sat on the seat behind him, put her arms around his waist, and leaned into his back.

32. He twisted the throttle again and rode off in the direction they were already headed.

33. They rode past people and buildings, over the bridge they had crossed,

34. and along the river, under streetlights on a quiet road that seemed to bend

35. like an arc around the city, which (to them) might as well have been the world,

36. during which time she held him more tightly until they reached their destination

37. where she let go—he felt how slowly she did—to dismount.

38. They shook (held) hands and said goodbye (he mumbled something about tomorrow),

39. and he watched her walk into the hotel until he could no longer see her, then rode away.

Chapter 18

1. Lashonda's memories were connected to the air around her more

2. than they were connected to anything else that memories are normally connected to—

3. a photograph, for example, a song, or an object—and it was the air itself that brought

4. the images of her memories but then also carried them away

5. on a breeze so that only the essence(s) of her memories were left for her to feel,

6. because all the images of her memories the air brought to her,

7. were distilled into only two feelings (feelings she could not describe but felt as distinct).

8. Feeling X, brought by a cool, crisp air which made her feel as if she were lying

9. on a bed of white sheets, in a white room, windows opened, her head on a soft, white pillow,

10. as the lightest draft blew in through white lace curtains and touched her face.

11. Feeling Y, brought by a sultry, oppressive air,

12. a layer of heat descending on the world which made her feel

13. as if she had awakened (between darkness and light) before her parents and sister,

14. and gone outside to travel the empty streets of her neighborhood,

15. maybe alone, maybe with her bicycle, as the sun came up

16. to cast the earth in an orange hue to match its temperature,

17. while every so often—turning a corner or passing an alleyway—

18. a cooler breeze (but still warm) drifted across her face to give her the illusion of a few sweet seconds of relief.

19. Her whole life, from the time she was born in the small, country hospital

20. to where she lived now and everything that happened in between

21. was either one memory (Feeling X) or the other (Feeling Y)

22. so that over time she only had to remember the cool, crisp air

23. or the sultry, oppressive air in order to remember everything—

24. the times she retied the shoelaces on one of her shoes but not the other,

25. songs she liked but did not know the names of,

26. strangers she spoke to on the bus who missed their stops and had to get off on the next, etc., etc.

27. And sometimes when she remembered them, they also brought something else:

28. the sense (Feeling Z?) that each was an eternal state she could stay in forever,

29. if for example, she did not know someone she loved and who also loved her,

30. although, on occasion, even that did not seem like enough.

Chapter 19

1. Lashonda didn't know what she was thinking when (on impulse)

2. she walked into the fan shop (across the street from her favorite brasserie)

3. where the old lady from Ishikawa prefecture who owned the shop

4. welcomed her ("ohayou goazimasu") and asked if she could help her find anything.

5. Lashonda said she was just looking, and the old lady continued to arrange fans

6. and other objects on the shelf behind the counter.

7. The fans she displayed depicted different scenes—a tiger under a tree, the sun over the ocean,

8. a bird flying near the moon—but there was one fan

9. that Lashonda could not stop looking at, decorated with two women,

10. one woman holding a bowl, the other woman hiding her face behind a fan of her own.

11. The old lady took the fan down from the shelf and lay it on the counter

12. then called Lashonda over (come) and explained the scene depicted on the fan

13. as the light from the bulbs in the shop (and from outside) seemed to close

14. into a sphere around them to also hear what she was saying.

15. This woman with the bowl (she pointed), was kidnapped by a group of samurai

16. and the woman with the fan (she moved her finger) is her sister, an onna-bugeisha,

17. who rode into the camp on a white horse to rescue her.

18. The little marks here are from the hooves of her horse.

19. The fan she is holding (she lifted her finger above it so Lashonda could see)

20. is called a tessen, a war fan, that could be hidden in her sash and used for fighting.

21. So this fan (she picked it up and turned her wrist to open it to its full display)

22. depicts the scene after the onna-bugeisha has been disarmed of her sword and before she is killed.

23. Lashonda bought the fan and took it home right away (skipping her coffee at the brasserie),

24. where she held it open in front of the mirror in her bedroom.

25. She had only fanned herself lightly and a few times before understanding that the fan

26. was too impressive to be treated as a common fan and flapped around

27. to cool the brows of any person who (quote-unquote) couldn't take the heat.

28. She cleared everything from her dresser and lay the fan open on the center.

29. She fell asleep that night knowing the fan was there, even though she couldn't see it,

30. but the next day she returned to the fan shop to buy a stand to put the fan on

31. because she wanted to see the fan while she was lying in bed

32. or from outside as she passed by her bedroom window on a cool spring (or any) day.

33. The old lady said she had to order a special stand for the fan,

34. because she only had one in the shop that she had to use for display.

35. Lashonda was disappointed to hear that it would take weeks for her to get the stand

36. but she ordered one and waited, hoping she would forget she had done so until it arrived.

Chapter 20

1. Lashonda's belonging was catalogued and placed into a small envelope:

2. one locket, although it could have been catalogued as two belongings:

3. one chain and one locket, but the person who catalogued the belonging

4. promised to take his daughter to the park (therefore the hurry),

5. where they would walk to the carousel and get something to eat or drink

6. or both and then stop in at the museum of natural history that was not far away

7. to see (again) the mastodon that raised its massive trunk

8. "even at night when no one was looking"—words his daughter always thought

9. like an uncontrollable tic in her brain when she saw it—

10. to the ceiling of the museum's entrance while at the same time pointing it to the floor.

11. She wanted to see (again) the spiders in the museum's insect zoo

12. and he wondered if today might not be the day his daughter stayed to watch

13. the tarantulas eat when the entomologist or entomologist's assistant

14. dropped a grasshopper or cricket in the eating vicinity

15. of the tarantulas which would sometimes eat and sometimes not

16. while the grasshopper or cricket seemed (scientifically) unaware of whatever fate awaited it,

17. but as the assistant (in this case) came out with the grasshoppers or crickets,

18. the daughter grabbed her father's hand and pulled him away,

19. telling him she was thirsty while he pretended to not notice the timing of her thirst,

20. saying out loud that it was a good idea to drink more water,

21. especially during such an unusually hot summer which had already wilted

22. the flowers he planted for his wife because he had forgotten to water them one time,

23. just once, but enough (?) to destroy the beauty of their little patch of land.

24. Something happened to him after he opened the locket

25. and before he put it in the small envelope, a sadness fell upon him—

26. not an overwhelming sadness, but a sadness that if he did not restrain would come to overwhelm him

27. so that he would cry (weep) at just the thought of his wife's dead flowers—his daughter would worry.

28. Maybe because the locket was a small, daughter-like object a girl might keep

29. as she grew older, a loose but certain connection to a *presentimento*

30. or *sense* or *raison d'etre*—he couldn't find the words in any language—

31. that not only made him feel as if he loved his wife and daughter more than he did yesterday,

32. but turned the notch on his feeling of love to a setting from where it could not be turned back,

33. to a new and never-before-felt feeling he held onto like a secret

34. that he didn't know how to share with anyone, not even them.

35. His daughter took a long drink from the water fountain near the entrance of the museum then told him she was ready to go home.

Chapter 21

1. Lashonda got up earlier than usual, on the morning her body was found,

2. to write down something she had thought of during the night after she was awakened

3. by the sound of the blind hitting the window ledge because of the strong wind

4. that had, overnight, unexpectedly come in from the east, and pushed dark clouds

5. over her vicinity; *note*: dark and heavy clouds that wore out the wind,

6. which gave up and left the clouds and the rain they brought with them to hang over Lashonda's house

7. (and not only hers) while she jotted down her thought: that just the idea—

8. she scribbled the word "lie" next to the word "idea" but crossed it out—that life had meaning

9. was enough to make up for the accumulation of a lifetime's worth of meaninglessness,

10. which she had accumulated over her lifetime and which, at first,

11. she could easily separate from the meaningfulness she had accumulated

12. but as she delved and delved (and delved further) she realized that perhaps it was not so easy, after all,

13. but then, as if of another mind, she realized she had been bamboozled,

14. hoodwinked, duped by the idea of a dichotomy that probably did not exist

15. and she supposed (as if of, etc.) that a single false idea might be the seed

16. from which all life, including the most beautiful life, was born.

17. She changed into her favorite white chiffon dress and gathered up

18. her manuscript of *The World That Destroyed the World* and walked out onto the wet grass in her bare feet.

19. She would use her bare hands to dig into the softened dirt and bury the papers between the two birch trees behind her house,

20. in the same spot she had buried the others, with her bare hands, but as she walked, and the rain pelted her body

21. she slipped and fell into a dip in the land where white flowers—*catharantus roseus*—grew,

22. and lay there, unable to move, soon unable to think, but while she could think,

23. the thought that came to her was not one of the thoughts she had practiced to think on her deathbed—

24. "no heavier than the tiny, unhatched egg of a hummingbird" or

25. "to tell you just tell me"—but the single word "no" and only once

26. which she managed to say with her last breath, as her eyes closed,

27. but so softly that it was as if she said nothing at all.

www.ingramcontent.com/pod-product-compliance
Lightning Source LLC
Chambersburg PA
CBHW030905170426
43193CB00009BA/741